J. M Daniaud

The wonders of arithmetic

or, The art of resolving, using only one figure, or by simple addition, all

rules of interest or discount, simple or complex, without having to divide,

acquired in ten minutes study

J. M Daniaud

The wonders of arithmetic
or, The art of resolving, using only one figure, or by simple addition, all rules of interest or discount, simple or complex, without having to divide, acquired in ten minutes study

ISBN/EAN: 9783744737227

Printed in Europe, USA, Canada, Australia, Japan

Cover: Foto ©Andreas Hilbeck / pixelio.de

More available books at **www.hansebooks.com**

THE WONDERS

OF

ARITHMETIC

OR

The Art of resolving, using only one figure, or by
simple Addition, all rules of Interest or Discount, simple or complex, without having
to divide, acquired in ten minutes
study.

STOCK OPERATIONS,

The Four Rules proved by a simple Addition,

as quick as thought.

BY

J. M. DANIAUD.

———————

MONTREAL :

EUSÈBE SENÉCAL, PRINTER AND PUBLISHER,

6, 8 and 10 St. Vincent Street,

———

1880

CHAPTER I.

Showing how all operations of Interest or Discount can be made without a Division..

If you want to find the interest on any sum, for one year, you shall multiply the capital by the rate, either simple or complex, that is with decimal fractions.

The rate is called simple when it is not followed by any fraction, as 1, 2, 3, 4, 5, 6, 7, 8, 9, etc.

The rate is called complex when it is followed by fractions, as 1.25, 1.75, 2.20, 2.25, 2.75, etc.

When you have multiplied the capital by a simple rate, you point off two decimals, by which you have divided by 100. The dollars stand to the left of the point and the cents to the right.

If you have a complex rate, you point off four decimals and the dollars stand to the left of the point, as above, and the cents to the right.

What is the interest on $4842 at 6 o/o for one year?

Example : $4842

6 o/o

$290.52   Answer : $290.52 cents.

What is the discount on $542 at 4 o/o for one year ?

Example : $542

4 o/o

$21.68   Answer : $21.68 cents.

What is the interest on $6424.10 at 5 o/o for one year ?

Example : $6424.10

5 o/o

321.2050   Ans.: $321.20 cts. 50 ou ½.

What is the interest on $248 at 4½ o/o for one year ?

Example : $248

4.50 o/o

12400
992

11.1600   Answer : $11.16 cents.

$23.223
8 o/o
_____
1857.84   Answer : $1857.84 cents.

How rules of Discount, simple or complex, can be made without a Division.

You add up all the figures of the capital, one after another, as many times as there are figures in it, begining with the unit, that is to say starting from right to left, and you add the amount carried from each addition to the following figure to the left, as if every figure was the column of an addition.

What is the interest or discount on $3422 at 4 o/o for one day?

Example : $3422.00
            380221   Answer $0.38 cents.

What is the interest on $4242 at 4 o/o for 21 days?

Example : $4242.00
            471332
               21—days
            _____
            471332
            942664
            _____
            9.897972   Answer : $9.89 79 that I will call as ₁$9.90, by leaving out the thousandths and adding a unit to the cents.

Proof by Division :
            4242
               4 o/o
            _____
            16968
               21—days
            _____
            16968
            33936
            _____
            356328 | 360
            3232 | _____
              3528   9.898
              2880
              0000   Answer : 9.90 cents.

But as you find yourself with more than ½ cent rest, you may add a unit to the cents and have the result: $9.90 cents. This result is the same as by the other operation which is much shorter and in which you do not have to divide.

What is the interest on $548.10 at 4 o/o for 4 days ?

```
Example:   54810.00
           6089998
                 4—days
           ————————————
           24.35.99.92   Answer: $0.24 cents.
```

Proof by Division:
```
           548.10
               4 o/o
           ————————
           219240
               4—days
           ————————
           876960 | 360
           1569   | ————
            1296    2436
            2160
            0000        Answer: $0.24 cents.
```
2nd example:

What is the interest on $4842 at 4 o/o for one day?
```
           4842.00
           537998   Answer: $0.54 cents.
```

You strike off, as before, the thousandths, and you add a unit to the cents.

Proof by Division:
```
           4842
              4 o/o
           ————————
           19368 | 360
           1368  | ————
            2880   53.8
            0000        Answer: $0.54 cents.
```

On the same capital at 4 o/o for 15 days :

Example: 4842.00
          537998
               15—days
          _____
          2689990
          537998
          _____
          8.069970   Answer : $8.07 cents.
Proof by Division :
          4842
             4 o/o
          _____
          19368
             15—days
          _____
          96840
          19368
          _____
          290520 | 360
            2520 | _____
            0000   8.07   Answer : $8.07 cents.
On the same capital at 6 o/o for one day :
   Example: 4842.00
             537998
             268999
          _____
             806997   Answer : $0.81 cents.
Proof by Division :
          4842
             6 o/o
          _____
          29052 | 360
           2520 | _____
           0000   80.7   Answer : $0.81 cents.
Same capital at 6 o/o for 20 days.
   Example: 4842.00
             537998
             268999
          _____
             806997
                20—jours
          _____
          16.139940   Answer : $16.14 cents.

Proof by Division :   4842
                           6 o/o
                        ─────────
                        29052
                            20—days
                        ─────────
                        581040 | 360
                        2210 |─────
                          504   16.14
                         1440   Ans. : $16.14 cents.

Other proof by Division :
                        4842
                          20—days
                        ─────────
                        96840 | 6
                          36 |─────
                           8   16.14
                          24   Answer : $ .14 cents.

What is the interest on $490 at 8 o/o for 45 days ?
    Example :   490.00
                 54443
                108886
                    45—days
                ─────────
                544430
                435544
                ─────────
                4.899870   Answer : $4.90 cents.

Same capital at 5 o/o for 120 days :
    Example :   490.00
                 54443
                 27221
                 13610
                     5 o/o
                ─────────
                68050
                  120—days
                ─────────
                136100
                68050
                ─────────
                8.166000   Answer : $8.17 cents.

Proof by Division:

```
      490
        8 o/o
      ─────
     3920
       45—days
      ─────
    19600
    15680
      ─────
   176400 | 360
     3240 | ─────
     0000    4.90
```

Answer : $4.90 cents.

Proof by Division:

```
      490
        5
      ─────
     2450
      120
      ─────
    49000
     2450
      ─────
   294000 | 360
      600 | ─────
     2400    8.166
     2400
      240
```

Answer : 8.17 cents.

Two more examples:

Capital :—
6848.00

760886—4 o/o	interest	for	one day
380443—2 o/o	"	"	"
190221—1 o/o	"	"	"
95110—½ o/o	"	"	"
47555—¼ o/o	"	"	"
23777—⅛ o/o	"	"	¡'

Capital :—
20000.00

```
2222222—4 o/o
1111111—2 o/o
 555555—1 o/o
 277777—½ o/o
 138888—¼ o/o
  69999—⅛ o/o
```

All these sums represent the interest for one day on the respective capitals of $6848 or 20000.

This operation shows what is the result of adding up the capital, from right to left, as many times as there are figures in it.

You must always add two ciphers to the capital, that will reduce it to cents, and will give six decimals to the sum; these decimals should be pointed off, to get the dollars to the left and the cents to the right of the point.

In the example on 6848.00 which you add up from right to left the result is 760886 ; this sum represents the interest at 4 o/o for one day ; 380443 must then represent the interest at 2 o/o, as it is one half of the first ; 190221 must represent 1 o/o.

In the example on 20000.00, there being only one

figure, 2, you cannot do *... rwise than to write 2 down under the ciphers and you have 2222222, for the interest at 4 o/o for one day ; 11,11111 for the interest at 2 o/o, and so forth.

It follows that when you have added up all the figures of a capital sum, as many times as there are figures, and adding to the figure next following on the left hand the amount carried from each addition, the result will be the interest at 4 o/o for one day, one half of such result will be the interest at 2 o/o, and soforth.

If then you want to find out the interest at 4 o/o on $20000 for 50 days, multiply the result of the addition from right to left of 20000 by 50 days and the product will give you the interest, after you have pointed off six decimals, the dollars standing tc the left of the point and the cents to the right.

Example : $20000.00
50 jours   2222222 4 o/o for one day
_____
111.11110   Answer : $111.11 cents.

The following is the way in which this adding up of the capital should be done to find out the interest at 4 o/o for one day :

Suppose you have to add upthe capital 4785. You begin by putting down the two necessary ciphers ; then you add up all the figures in the capital, one after another, taking care to add to the following figure to the left, the amount carried from each addition and the sum will give you the interest at 4 o/o for one day.

Example : '4785,00
531664—4 o/o for one day

The sum 531664 has been obtained as follows : 5 and 8 are 13 and 7=20 and 4=24, I set down 4 and carry 2 which I add to the 5, I say : 2 and 5 are 7 and 8=15 and 7=22 and 4=26, I set down 6 and carry 2 which I add again to the 5 (so much for the two ciphers) and I say : 2 and 5 are 7 and 8=15 and 7=22 and 4=26, I set down 6 and carry 2 ; 2 carried and 8 are 10 and 7=17 and 4=21, I set down 1 and carry 2 ; 2 carried and 7 are 9 and 4=13, I set down 3 and carry 1; 1 carried and 4 are 5, I set down 5.

The sum of this addition of all the figures in the capital is: 531664, and this sum represents 4 o/o interest for one day on a capital of 4785, or $0.53 and some thousandths.

It only remains to multiply by the number of days to find the interest wanted, if for more than one day.

I should be stated here that the thousandths must be included in multiplication of the addition by number of days.

You will therefore multiply 531664 by the number of days the capital has been bearing interest, because if you should multiply 53 cents only, the result for one day, there would be a large difference, if for a considerable number of days. It is therefore necessary to multiply the whole sum, whenever you have more than one day's interest.

FURTHER EXPLANATION OF THE ADDITION.

You must have noticed that in adding up the capital, it is necessary to go back three times to the last figure on account of the two cyphers following the capital. In the same manner when there are cyphers in the body of numbers, you must go back once more than the number of cyphers on the figure next following them on the left hand side.

Let us take as a capital to be added up the following: 200242, I will put down the two cyphers after the capital, and I will add up as before, but in going back three times on the figure 2 which is the last one of the capital, on account of the two cyphers by which it is followed.

And as to the two cyphers in the body of the number, following the figure 2, the first one of the capital, I add the figures 2, 2, 4, 2, which are 10, I set down aught and carry 1; 1 carried and 2 are 3 and 2=5 and 4=9 and 2=11, I set down 1 and carry 1; 1 carried and 2 are 3 and 2=5 and 4=9 and 2=11, I set down 1 and carry 1; 1 carried and 2 are 3 and 2=5 and

4=9, I set down 9 and carry aught; I begin again with the 2 (the first figure of the capital) and I say: 2 and 2 are 4, I set down 4 and carry aught; as I have nothing more to add for the ciphers, I set down 2 for each of them and also for the first figure of the capital.

The sum of this addition is 22249110. And if I point off six decimals, I will have 22.24, which I will put down as $22.25 cents interest for one day, leaving off the thousandths unless I should multiply by the number of days my capital has been bearing interest.

If I want to find out the interest at 6 o⁄o on this capital which gave me as interest at 4 o⁄o : 22249110, I shall take one half of that number, and add it up to the same, and that will give me the interest at 6 o⁄o : it will then only be necessary to multiply by the number of days stated and having pointed off six decimals, I will have the $ to the left and the cents and thousandths to the right of the point.

```
Example :   22249110—4 o⁄o
            11124555
            _____

            33373665
                70—days
            _____

        2336.156550
```

Answer : $2336.16 cents.

We have in this way, as the interest asked for $2336.16 cents and some thousandths which are left off in the final result of the operations.

It is well to strike off the thousandths, and add one to the cents, (as I said before) because in the final result only cents need be accounted for.

The addition of the capital can be made in various ways; it can be made by putting down the capital five times echellons by respecting every figure, putting down five times that representing the units, five times that representing the tenths, five times that representing the hundredths, etc., etc.

The sum of the addition will every time represent the interest at 4 o⁄o for one day.

What is the interest on $845 at 4 o|o for 40 days ?

Example :   845
      845
      845
      845
      845
     —————
      9388795—4 o|o for one day
        40—days
     —————
    3.7555.18.00

Answer : $3.75.55 i. e. $3.76 cents.

Other example by repeating the figures of the same capital on $845 :

      55555
      44444
      88888
     —————
      9388795—4 o|o interest for one day
        40—days
     —————
    3.75551800
        Answer : $3.76 cents.

The result is the same for both operations. With both these methods, it is necessary to point off eight decimals in the sum, to have the $ to the left and the cents to the right of the point. Here is the proof of the two preceeding rules by addition of the capital.

Example : $ 845.00
      93887—4 o|o for one day
       40—days
     —————
    3.755480   Answer : $3.76 cents.

Proof by division :   845
                         4 o/o
                       _____
                       3380
                       40—days
                       _____
                       135200 | 360
                       2720 | ____
                       2000   3.75
                       200   Answer : $3.76 cents.

With the method of adding up the capital, the operations are considerably shorter ; and when you have acquired the habit of adding up the capital as we have just been doing, you will be able to calculate interest or discount as quick as thought.

We have seen that the operations can be made by adding up all the figures of the capital in order to find the interest at 4 o/o for one day. We propose now to show how the interest can be found for the number of days the capital has been bearing interest. If you multiply the capital by the number of days and if you add up the figures of the result, in the same way as above, you will have the interest for the number of days given.

Example of the preceeding rules ;

  .845   Proof: 845.00
    40 days   93887
  _____   40—days
  33800   _____
  3.7554   Answer : $3.76 cents.   3.755480
                                         Answer : $3.76

Other example with a capital of 3.241 at 4 o/o for 12 days :

  3241   Proof : 3241.00
   12—days   3601.10
  _____   12—days
  6482   _____
  3241   720220
                                         360110
  _____   _____
  38892 addition.
  4.3210   Answer : $4.32 cents.   4.321320
                                         Answer : 4.32

Proof bv division :

```
    3241
       4 o/o
  ───────
   12964
      12
  ───────
   25928
   12964
  ───────
  155568 | 360
    1156 | ───
     768   4.32
      48            Answer : $4.32 cents.
```

After the multiplication by the number of days, four decimals only require to be pointed off in the result, on account of the ciphers being omitted.

And if you will consider carefully the foregoing remark, you will find that it is not necessary to add the two ciphers, when the multiplication takes place before the addition.

Example :
```
            845
             40 days
         ───────
         33800
         33800
         33800
         33800
        33800
        ─────────
        3.75551800
            Answer : $3.76 cents.
```

In the foregoing operation, the same result is arrived at. But with this last method, it is always necessary to point off eight decimals in order to have the $ to the left and the cents to the right of the point.

Other example : 845
                 40 days

                 33800
                 00000
                 88888
                 33333
                 33333

                 3.75551800   Answer : $3.76 cents.

The result remains the same, after pointing off eight decimals.

All these rules give the interest at 4 o/o ; and when the interest at 4 o/o on any capital is once arrived at, it is easy to get at every rate. Take one half of 4 o/o you have 2 o/o ; take one half of 2 o/o you have 1 o/o.

When you have the 1 o/o rate, you multiply by the rate given and then by the number of days; and you get the interest asked for after pointing off four decimals, if you have not added the two ciphers.

Every time you add those two ciphers to the right of the capital, you must point off six decimals.

But if the rates are complex, you must point off two more decimals in the result.

If you want to operate on any rate of interest, you can do so by getting first the 1 o/o interest which is ¼ of the 4 o/o i. e. of the sum of the addition from right to left, which represents the 4 o/o rate.

Example :   3421.00 à 5 o/o for 21 days
            380110
            190055
             95027
                    5 o/o

            475135
                21—days

            475135
            950270

            9.977835   Answer : $9.98 cents.

32 cents.

of days, four the result, on

foregoing re- ry to add the place before

esult is ar- always ne- to have the le point.

All rules can also be made in this way : multiply first the capital by the number of days, then by the rate ; take ¼ of the result and add it up as many times as there are figures in it ; point off four decimals in the sum and you will have the $ to the left and the cents to the right of the point.

What is the interest on 8422 at 3 o/o for 48 days?

Example :   8422   Capital.
48—days

```
67376
33688
```

```
404256
    3 o/o
```

ₑ

```
121276R—total.
606384
```
to be added up 303192—¼ of the total,

```
33.6878    Answer : 33.69
```

Proof :   842200
935776—4 o/o
467888
233944—unit or ¼
      3 o/o

```
701832
  48—days
```

```
5614656
2807328
```

```
33.687936        Answer : 33.69
```

In this operation,the capital has been multiplied by the number of days, and then by rate ; the result has been 1212768, ¼ of this sum is 303192; the addition from right to left of the figures of the last sum, furnishes, after the pointing off of four decimals, the amount 33.68.78. A unit is added to the cents and the thousandths left out.

Other example on the same capital.

8422	Other example :	8422
48		48

67376		67376
33688		37688

404256		404256
3 o/o		449171
		224585
		112292

1212768	
1347517	33.6877
673758	
33,6879 Answer : 33.69.	Answer : 33.69.

In this operation, the capital has been multiplied by the number of days ; then by the rate, and the result was a total sum of 1212768. This result has been added up from right to left, and the answer has been one fourth of the sum of this addition.

Proof by division :

$$8422$$
$$3 \; o/o$$

$$25266$$
$$48 \; days$$

$$202128$$
$$101064$$

1212768	360
1327	
2476	33.688
3168	
2880	
0000	Answer : 33.69.

The rule to be followed as to the number of decimals to be pointed off is the following : For the capital, two, for the simple rate, two, for the two ciphers that follow the capital, two, and if the rate is complex, for the decimals in the rate, two, making all told eight decimals, if are combined in the operation all these conditions.

Other method of operating by the unit.
Example . 7424 à 7.50 for 50 days.
```
    7424.00
    824887—4 o/o
    412443—2 o/o
    206221—1 o/o or unit.
      7.50
    ─────────
    1031105
    1443547
    ─────────
    154665750
        50—days
    ─────────
    77.33287500          Answer : 77.32 cents.
```
¹ All operations can be made with the unit, let the rate be complex or not.

The unit always represents 1 o/o interest for one day, if the capital has not been multiplied by number of days; but if on the contrary, the unit will represent 1 o/o interest for the number of days the capital has been multiplied by, and it will only be required to multiply by the rate.

We will give two examples of that below.

What is the interest on 743 at 5.25 for 43 days ?
```
    743.00               632300
    82554                702554
    41277                351277
    20638—unit           175638—unit
       43—days               9 o/o
    ─────────            ─────────
    61914                1580742
    82552                   22— days
    ─────────            ─────────
    887434               3161484
      5.25- -rate        3161484
    ─────────            ─────────
    4437170              34.776324
    1774868                 Answer : 34.78 cents.
    4437170

    ─────────
    4.6590263.    Answer : 4.66.
```

Proof by division :   7 13
                        5.25

                        3715
                        1486
                        3715

                    390075
                        43—days

                 1170225
                 1560300

                16773225 | 360
                 2373
                 2132   4.6592
                  3322
                   825
                   105   Answer : 4. 66.

Other examples :
What is the interest on 4842 at 4 o/o for one day ?
    484200   Proof by division :
    0.537998   4842
Answer : 0.54 cents.   4 o/o

                  19369 | 360
                  1368
                   2880 538
                   0000
                 Answer : 0.54 cents.

Same capital at 4 o/o for 15 days :
Example :   4842.00   Proof by division :
          537998   4842
            15—days   4 o/o

        2689990   19368
        537998   15— davs

        8.069970   96840
Answer : $8.07 cents.   19368

                  290520

```
290520 | 360
  2520 |  ———
  0000   8.07
```
Answer : $8.07 cents.

Same capital at 6 o/o for 20 days

Example :   484200   Proof by division.
```
        537998—4 o/o              4842
        268999—2 o/o                20—days
        ———                     ———
        806997                    96840 | 6
            20—days               36    |  ———
        ———                        8      16.14
     16.139940                    24
```
ℓ Answer : $16.14 cents.   Answer : 16.14 cents.

What is the interest on $490 at 8 o/o for 45 days?

Example :   490.00
```
              54443—4 o/o
            108886—double or 8 o/o.
                45—days
            ———
           544430
           435544
           ———
           4.899870
```
Answer : $4.90 cents.

Proof by division :   490
```
                                    8 o/o
                                 ———
                                 3920
                                   45—days
                                 ———
                                19600
                                15680
                                ———
                               176400 | 360
                                 3240 |  ———
                                 0000   4.90
```
Answer : 4.90 cents.

Same capital at 5 o/o for 120 days.
Example :   490.00
              54443
              13610—unit or both together 5 o/o.
            ───────
              68053
                120—days

            ───────
            1361060
              68053
            ───────
            8.166360   Answer : $8.17 cents.
      Proof by division :   490
                              5 o/o
                             ────
                             2450
                              120—days

                             ────
                             4900
                             2450
                            ─────
                            294000 │ 360
                               600 │────
                              2400   8.166
                              2400
                               240 Answer : 8.17 cents.
What is the interest on 2333 a 5 o/o for 22 days ?
      Example :   Proof :
      2333.00   2333
      259221—4 o/o   5 o/o
      129610—2 o/o   ─────
       64805—1 o/o or unit'   11665
          5 o/o   22—days
      ───────   ─────
      324025   23330
          22—days   23330
      ───────   ──────
      648050   256630 │ 360
      648050   463 │────
      ───────   1030   7.128
      7.128550   3100
Answer : $7.13 cents.   220
                                  Answer : $7.13 cents.

What is the interest on 745 at 7 o/o for 15 days?

Example:

Making together 7 o/o

745.00
82776—4 o/o
41388—2 o/o
20694—1 o/o
———
144858
    15—days
———
724290
144858
———
2172870
Answer: 2.17 cents.

Proof:

745
 7 o/o
———
5215
15—days
———
26075
5215
———
78225 | 360
622 | ———
2625 | 2.17
105 | Ans.: 2.17 cents.

Other example at 7 o/o for 20 days on a capital of 48948.20.

Making together 7 o/o

48948.20.00
543868885—4 o/o
271934442—2 o/o
135967221—1 o/o
———
951770548
    20—days
———
190.35410960
Answer: 190.35 cents.

Proof:

48948.20
 7 o/o
———
34263740
20—days
———
685274800 | 360
3252 | ———
1274 | 190.3541
1948 |
1480 |
400 |
Ans.: $190.35 cents.—40

You may see that the result arrived at is always the same as with a division, and the operation is much shorter as it is easier and more convenient to add up and to multiply than to divide.

With this method you will save much time, because you won't have the trouble to find out how many times 360 is in any given number; and when you have acquired the habit of adding up the capital from right to left, you will be able to do all rules of interest or discount as quickly as you can write down the figures.

RULE AT 6 o/o.

In all rules at 6 o/o, where the number of days is divisible by 6 without leaving a fraction, the capital may be multiplied by the figure obtained as quotient.

Example :—What is the interest on 745 at 6 o/o for 42 days ?

745	745	for 12 days
7	2	

5.215	1.490
Answer : 5.21	Ans. : 1.49 cents.

What is the interest on 4323 at 6 o/o for 48 days ?

Example :   4323
                    48

34,584   Answer : 34.58

Proof: 4323.00   Proof :   745.00
                480332   82776
                240166   41388

              720498   124164
                    48   12—days

            5763984   248328
            2881992   124164

          34.583904   1.489968
Answer : 34.58   Answer : 1.49 cents.
Proof by division :   By divisor 6.
            745   745
              6 o/o   42—days

            4470   1490
              42—days   2980

            8940   31290 | 6
          17880   12   ———
                                                  9   5.215
        187740 | 360   30
        774   ———   Answer : 5.21 cents.
        540   5.21
        180   Answer : 5.21

The same rule applies to the 4 o/o interest where the number of days is divisible by 9. Examples are given below.

It is clear that, as 42 divided by 6 gives 7, I multiply 745 by 7 and point off three decimals in the result in order to have the $ to the left of the point and the cents to the right.

What is the interest on 745 at 4 o/o for 36 days?

Example :   745
               4
        —————
       2.980   Answer : 2.98

Other example at 4 o/o for 72 days on a capital of
       3248
         8
     ————
    25.984   Answer : 25.98

Proof by addition of   Proof by division :
  the capital :   745
  745.00   4 o/o
  82776   ————
    36—days   2980
  ———   36—days
  496656   ————
  248328   17880
  ———   8940
  2.979936   ————
  Answer : 2.98   107280 | 360
                        3528 | ————
                        2880   2.98
                        0000
            Answer : 2.98 cents.

Rates can also be computed with the capital.

What is the interest on $840 at 6 o/o for 70 days?

Example :   840—4 o/o ⎱
           420—2 o/o ⎰ giving together 6 o/o.

        1260
         70—days
       ————
      88200—to be added up
     9.7998   Answer : $9.80 cents.

rest where the
ples are given

s 7, I multiply
a the result in
point and the

r 36 days?

a capital of

f by division :
45
 4 o/o
—
80
36—days
—
80
0
—
30 | 360
3 |
30   2.98
)0
 2.98 cents.
pital.
r 70 days?
ether 6 o/o.

80 cents.

Proof by putting down the capital in echellons :

1260	Proof: 840.00
1260	93332—4 o/o
1260	46666—2 o/o
1260	
1260	139998
	70—days
13999860	
70—days	9.799860
	Answer: 9.80
9.79990200 Answer : 9.80	

Other example at 7 o/o on a capital of 840, for the same number of days :

$$\left.\begin{array}{l}\text{Capital—840—4 o/o}\\\text{Half—420—2 o/o}\\\text{Quarter—210—1 o/o}\end{array}\right\}\text{Together 7 o/o}$$

1470
70—days

102900—to be added up
11.4332   Answer : 11.43 cents.

Proof :

840.00
$$\left.\begin{array}{l}83332\text{—4 o/o}\\46666\text{—2 o/o}\\23333\text{—1 o/o}\end{array}\right\}\text{together 7 o/o}$$

163331
70—days

11.433170   Answer : 11.43 cents.

In the 6 o/o rule we have taken one half of 840, which we have added to the latter sum; and we have multiplied the total 1260 by the number of days given, the result was 88200, we have added up the figures of this result as many times as there are figures in it; we have pointed off four decimals (as the two ciphers were not added), and we have had for an answer: 9.7998, that we called 9.80 leaving out the thousandths and adding one to the cents.

But we know that the addition can be made by putting down the capital in echellons in the manner we have indicated. This is tantamount to adding up from right to left the figures in the capital.

Some examples will be given here:

EXAMPLES BY ECHELLONS.

What is the interest on 840 at 7 o/o for 70 days?

$$
\left.\begin{array}{l}
840\text{—}4\ o/o \\
420\text{—}2\ o/o \\
210\text{—}1\ o/o
\end{array}\right\} \text{together 7 o/o}
$$

```
    1470
    1470
    1470
    1470
    1470
  ─────────
  16333170
       70—days
  ─────────────
11.43321900   Answer : 11.43 cents.
```

Other example :

```
    00000
    77777
    44444
    11111
  ─────────
  16333170
       70—days
  ──────────
11.43321900
       Answer : 11.43
```

Proof :

```
    840.00
    93332—4 o/o
    46666—? o/o
    23333—1 o/o
  ────────────
   163331
       70—days
  ──────────
11.433170
    Answer : 11.43 cts.
```

the two ciphers
for an answer:
the thousandths

an be made by
n the manner we
adding up from

3.

for 70 days?

· 7 o/o

cents.

Proof:

0.00
3332—4 o/o
5666—2 o/o
3333—1 o/o

3331
70—days

5170
wer: 11.43 cts.

Other proof:

> 840—Capital
> 70—days
>
> ———
>
> 58800—to be added up and struck off
> 65331—4 o/o
> 32665—2 o/o
> 16332—1 o/o
>
> ———
>
> 11.4328   Answer: 11.43 cents.

Other example at 8 o/o for 41 days on a capital of

> 42231.00
> 4692332
>   2—Multip. or doubling the sum
>
> ———
>
> 9384664
> 41—days
>
> ———
>
> 9384664
> 37538656
>
> ———
>
> 384.771224   Answer: 384.771224

Proof by division:

> 42231
>   8 o/o
>
> ———
>
> 337848
> 41—days
>
> ———
>
> 337848
> 1351392
>
> ———
>
> 13851768 | 360
> 3051
> 1717   384.77
> 2776
> 2568
>   48   Answer: 384.77 cents.

In all these rules by putting down the capital by
echellons it is necessary to point off eight decimals in
order to have the $ to the left of the point and the
cents to the right.

All operations can be made by one figure only,
either with the addition or with the division.
What is the interest on 840 at 4 o/o for 70 days ?

ι Example :   840
               7—regulating figure

            5880—sum to be struck off
          , 6531—addition
          1680 —double capital

          23331
            4 o/o rate

          93324
            70—days

       6.532680   Answer : 6.53 cents.

Other example à 8 o/o on the same capital for 50
days.
        · 840
             7—regulating figure

          5880—sum to be struck off
          6531—addition
          1680 —double capital

          23331—unit
            50—days

        1166550
           8 o/o rate

       9.332400   Answer : 9.33 cents.

Proof by addition :
840
70—days
_____
58800
6.5331   Answer : 6.53 cents.

Proof by addition of the figures in the capital, at 8 o/o
840.00
93332
186664
50 days
_____
9.333200   Answer : 9.33 cents.

Other proof :   840
50—days
_____
42000 .
4.6666—4 o/o.
2
_____
9.3332—8 o/o.
Answer : 9.33 cents.

We call the figure 7, regulating figure, because it can be made use of in all operations. In fact, it furnishes the unit, in this way : the capital is multiplied by 7 ; the result of this is added up as many times as there are figures in it, as we have done before ; then the capital is multiplied by 2, and the result put down under the sum of the previous addition, beginning under the tenths. The total on which the addition has been made and which is the result of the multiplication by 7 is then struck off, and the sum of the addition is added to the result of the multiplication of the capital by 2 or double capital.

It is always necessary in these operations to point off eight decimals in order to have the $ to the left of the point and the cents to the right.

Other example on the same capital of 840 at 5.25 o/o for 82 days :

840
7—regulating figure

5880—to be struck off
6531—addition
1680 —double capital.

23331—unit
5.25—rate

116655
46662
116655

12248775
82—days

24497550
97990200

10.04399550   Answer : 10.04 cents.

PROOF.

84000   840
93332—4 o/o   5.25
46666—2 o/o
23333—1 o/o   4200
5.25—rate   1680
                                     4200
116665
46666   441000
116665   82—days

12249825   882000
    82—days   3528000

24499650   36162000 | 360
97998600   1620 |
                                          180   10.04
10.04485650   Answer : 10.04 cents.
Answer : 10.04 cents.

We must here point off eight decimals on account of the two decimals on the rate with this method.

Nota. — Whenever the rate is simple, six decimals are pointed off, and eight decimals whenever the rate is complex.

As the rule at 6 o/o is of the most frequent occurrence with traders, I will give some more examples of it.

What is the interest on 4800 at 6 o/o for 50 days?

Example :
```
      4800.00
      533332—4 o/o
      266666—2 o/o
      ───────
      799998
          50—days
      ──────────
   39,999900      Answer : $39.99.
```

cents.

Which we will call $40, leaving out the thousandths and adding one to the cents.

What is the interest on 2323 at 6 o/o for 16 days ?

days

360
───
10.04
10.04 cents.

Example :	Proof :
232300	2323—capital.
258110—4 o/o	16—days
129050—2 o/o	─────
───────	13938
387160	2323
16—days	─────
─────────	37168—to be added up
2322960	41295—4 o/o
387160	20647—2 o/o
─────────	─────
6.194560	6.1942

Réponse : $6.19 cents.   Answer : 6.19.

The 6 o/o rule can be made in the following manner :

Example : On a capital of 840 for 82 days.

```
       840                    Proof by division :
         6—o/o                       840
      ——                              82—days
    5040—to be struck off           ——
    5599—addition                   1680
     840 —capital                   6720
    ——                              ——
   13999                           68880 | 6
      82—days                          8  ——
  ——                                  28
   27998                              48
  111992                    Answer : 11.48 cents.
```

1147918   Answer : 11.48 cents.

The operation has been done this way : the capital
has been multiplied by 6, the result was 5040, this
latter sum we have added up as many times as there
are figures in it ; the sum was 5599, under this we have
put down the capital, beginning under the tenths, as
we have seen done with the regulating figure 7, with
this difference that this time we do not double the capital ; then we have multiplied by the number of days
given and we have pointed off five decimals (this is a
general rule for this method).

The same rule by the divisor 7 is given below :

```
Example :  840           Proof :  840
             7                     932—4 o/o
          ——                       466—2 o/o
          5880                    ——
          6531                    1398
          1680                      82—days
        ——                       ——
         23331                    2796
             6 o/o              11184
        ——                       ——
        139986                   11,4636
            82            Answer : 11.46 cents.
       ——
       279972
      1119888
       ——11.478752        Answer : 11.48 cents.
```

With this kind of proof, it would be necessary to add one to the sum of the addition from right to left, in order to get at the same result. Some examples are given below.

What is the interest on 450 at 6 o/o for 50 days ?

Example :		Proof :
450		450
7		499—4 o/o
——		——
3150		500
3499		250
900 —double capital		——
——		750
12499		50
6 o/o		——
——		3.7500
74994		Answer : 3.75 cents.
50—days		

3.749700   Answer : 3.75 cents.

For the *modus operandi* see first rule by the divisor 7.

In the proof, the addition has been made from right to left and one added ; I had in this way 500, as the 4 o/o and 250, as 2 o/o interest which gives 750 ; I multiply 750 by 50, and I have for an answer 3.75.

The following rule is generally unsed by accountants ; it is to find out the 6 o/o interest for 60 days on any capital, by pointing off two decimals.

What is the interest on $450 for 60 days at 6 o/o.
Answer : 4.50 cents.
Proof by division :   450
                         60
                         ——
                    27000 | 6
                       30 | ——
                           | 4.500
                Answer : 4.50 cents.

Other proof :
```
           45000
           49999
           24999
          ───────
           74998
              60
          ───────
         4.499880        Answer : 4.50 cents.
```

What is the interest on 450 at 4 o⁄o for 90 days ?

Answer : 4.50 cents.

Proof by division :
```
                          450
                           )0
                        ─────────
                        40500 | 9
                        45    | ─────
                              | 4.500
```

Answer : 4.50 cents.

This, as you may see, gives a correct answer, but these two last rules, by pointing off two decimals, can only be applied to interest for 60 or 90 days. When the interest at 6 o⁄o for 60 days is found, you may easily find it for 30 days, for 15, for 7½, etc. If for more than 60 days, you may add the 7½, 15, or 30 days interest, etc.

In the 6 o⁄o and 4 o⁄o rules, three decimals are pointed off, because a cipher is left out in the divisor; it should be 60 or 90 instead of 6 or 9 ; to equalize the matter it should be necessary to strike off one figure in the dividend, if this has not been done, there is one decimal more in the quotient, three instead of two.

It follows that the capital had better be multiplied by the number of days, and divided by 6, if it is at 6 o⁄o, or divided by 9, if it is at 4 o⁄o.

This last method may be applied to any number of days.

RULE FOR MAKING ALL OPERATIONS WITH THE
DIVISOR 9.

What is the interest on $840 at 3 o/o for 50 days?

Example :　　　 840 　　　　　 Proof: 31500
　　　　　　　 3 o/o 　　　　　　　　 3.4999
　　　　　　　 ———　　　　 Answer : 3.50 cents.
　　　　　　　 2520
　　　　　　　 50—days
　　　　　　　 ———

total.—126000
half.— 63000
quarter.— 31500 | 9
　　　　　　 45 | ———
　　　　　 3.500　　 Answer : 3.50 cents.

OTHER PROOF.

84000 　　　　　　　　　 840
93332 　　　　　　　　　 3 o/o
466o6 　　　　　　　　 ———
23333 　　　　　　　　 2520
3 o/o 　　　　　　　　 50—days
———　　　　　　　　 ———
69999 　　　　　　 126000 | 360
50—days 　　　　　 1800 | ———
———　　　　　　　 0000　 3.50
3.499950

Answer : 3.50 cents.　　　　　 Answer : 3.50 cents.

In these operations with the divisor 9, the result of
the multiplication by the rate and by the number of
days, should be divided first by 4 and then by 9.

Remark.—The addition of the capital from right to
left, as we have previously done, is equal to the ninetieth part; if this ninetieth part is divided by four, we
have the three hundred and sixtieth part, or the unit,
or the interest for one day.

If we should multiply the capital by the number of
days before dividing by 9, we will have as quotient
the interest at 4 o/o, for the number of days the capital
has been multiplied by.

If the capital is divided before the multiplication by
the number of days, we shall follow the division up to
three decimals ; and after the multiplication by the

number of days, we shall point off six decimals in order to have the $ to the left and the cents to the right of the point.

What is the interest on 450 at 4 o/o for 50 days?

Example :	450		Proof :	45000
	50			49999
				.50
	22500	9		
	45			2.499950
Answer : 2.50.		2.500	Answer : 2.50 cents.

What is the interest on 5555 à 4 o/o for 80 days?

Example :	5555		Proof :	555500
	80			617220
				80
	444400	9		
	84			49.377600
	34	49.377	Answer : 49.38 cts.
	70		
	70		
	7		

Answer : 49.38 cents.

Proof by addition.

5555	5555
80	5555
	5555
444400	5555
49.3776	5555
Answer : 49.38 cents.	
	61721605
	80

Answer : 49.38 cents.—49.37728400

What is the interest on 752 at 4 o/o for 50 days?

Example :   Proof by addition.

Proof by addition :	752		752.00
752	50		83554
50			50
	37600	9	
37600	16		4.177700
4.1776	70	4.177	Ans. 4.18 cts.
Answer : 4.18.	70	Ans. 4.18.

It will be seen from the proofs we have made of the preceeding rules, that the addition from right to left, is equivalent to division by 9.

Everybody knows that the general rule is to compute interest for a certain number of days; it is only by exception that it is computed for a month or for ¼, ½ or ¾ of a year.

It is therefore necessary to use a division in order to make all operations of interest or discount.

With this system, division is abolished, and advantageously replaced by the addition from right to left; it is always easier and more convenient to add up than to divide.

CHAPTER II.

RULES FOR THE STOCK OPERATIONS MOST IN USE.

If the 5 o/o bonds are at $75, what capital may be necessary to acquire an income of $650 ?

Example:
$$\begin{array}{r}
650 \\
2 \\
\hline
1300 \\
75 \\
\hline
6500 \\
9100 \\
\hline
9750,0
\end{array}$$ Answer: 9750.

This operation is done by doubling the income wanted and then multiplying by the quotation.

One decimal is pointed off in the result, which is dividing by ten, and the $ stand to the left and the cents to the right of the point.

2

Proof by the rule of three.
   Example :   5 : 75 : : 650 : X
                      75

                3250
                4550

             48750 | 5
              37 |
               25   9750
                ..   Answer : 9750.

In this operation, the 650 income has been multiplied by the quotation, 75, and the result divided by 5; this means that as $5 is the income derived from $75, what capital is the $650 to be derived from ?

The above operation is made by the rule of three simple, and it reads thus :

5 is to 75 as 650 is to X.

We will now reverse the preceeding rule and ask : if 75 give 5 per cent. income, how much will 9750 giv e?

    Example :   75 : 5 : : 9750 : X
                      5

             48750 | 75
              375 |
              000   650 :
                   Answer : $650.

If 75 yields 8, how much will 5625 yield ?

   Example :   75 : 8 : : 5625 : X
                    8

            45000 |. 75
            000 |
               600 Ans. : 600.

    8 : 75 : : 600 : X
          75

        3000
        4200

        45000

```
45000 |. 8
   50 |____
   20   5625
   40
   00   Answer: 5625.
```

PROOF OF THE FOUR RULES.

Addition :　324—9　　Subtraction :　84216—3
　　　　　 632—2　　　　　　　　　 32214
　　　　　 784—1　　　　　　　　　 _____
　　　　　 _____　　　　　　　　　 52002—3
　　　　 1740—3—3

Multiplication :　432—9
　　　　　　　　 17—8
　　　　　　　　 _____
　　　　　　　　 3024—9
　　　　　　　　 432
　　　　　　　　 _____
　　　　　　　　 7344—9

Division =3 =4787 |　34　=　7
　　　　　　　 138 |　_____　=3
　 4787　　　　 270　14079=3
　　 14　　　　 320
　 ____　　　　 14
　 4773

PROOFS EXPLAINED.

To prove the addition, it is necessary to add up all the figures of every number once, and reduce each sum to one figure. The first number gives 9, as 9 is only one figure, we will put it down opposite the number. The second number is 632, which gives 11: we add up this two figures and have 2, which we put down opposite. The third number is 784, the figures added up give 19, we reduce to one figure and have 1, which we put opposite. The three figures 9, 2, 1 added up and reduced to one figure give 3. And the addition of all the figures in the sum, after reducing to one, must also give the figure 3.

This proof may also be made by adding up the figures of every number as if they were written in one horizontal line and forming but one number, passing over the figure 9 whenever it is found and reducing the sum to one figure.

The proof of the subtraction is made by adding up the minuend and reducing to one figure, as for addirion, we have therefore 21, which reduced to one figure, gives 3. Then the subtrahend is added up with the remai-'er and we find again 21 which reduced to one figure, .eaves again the same figure 3, the figure being the same the operation is proved to be correct.

In the multiplication, the multiplicand 432 is added up and gives 9, which is only one figure and needs no reducing; the multiplier is also added up and gives 8, I multiply by 8 and I have 72, I reduce to one figure and I have 9. The result of the multiplication is then added up and gives 18, which reduced to one figure gives 9, the two figures being equal, the operation is proved to be correct.

In the division, the dividend is added up and if there is a remainder it is deducted from the dividend.

Example 4787, the remainder 14 deducted, we have 4773, add up once every figure in the latter number, you have 21, reduce to one figure, you have 3. Add up the divisor 34, you have 7, add up also the quotient 14079, you have 21, reduce to one figure, you have 3, multiply 7 by 3, you have 21, which reduced to one figure, gives 3.

The figure given by the dividend being the same as the one given by the multiplication of the two others numbers, the operation is correct.

It is not necessary to divide the sum of additions by divisor 9, to prove an addition : all that is wanted is to reduce to one figure, that being equivalent to the remainder after a division by number 9.

Example : add up every figures of 789654, you have 39, reduce to one figure, you have 3.

By division, if vou divide 39 by 9, you have 4 : 4 times 9 is 36, which deducted from 39, leaves 3.

Thus, without division, the same result is arrived at, and operations can be proved as quick as thought.

In adding up, the figure 9 may be passed over; that is to say, it is not necessary to add it up with the other figures.

MULTIPLICATION TABLE.

1	2...	3...	4...	5...	6...	7...	8...	9...	10
2	4...	6...	8. ·	10...	12...	14...	16...	18...	20
3	6...	9...	12...	15...	18...	21...	24...	27...	30
4	8...	12...	16...	20...	24...	28...	32 ..	36...	40
5	10...	15...	20...	25...	30...	35...	40...	45...	50
6	12...	18...	24...	30...	36...	42...	48...	54...	60
7	14...	21...	28...	35...	42...	49...	56...	63...	70
8	16...	24...	32...	40...	48...	56...	64 ..	72...	80
9	18...	27...	36...	45...	54...	63...	72...	81...	90
10	20...	35...	40...	50...	60...	70...	80...	90...	100

At 4 o/o Multiply the capital by the number of days, add up from right to left and point off four decimals.

At 5 o/o Multiply the capital by the number of days, add up from right to left, add one fourth.

At 6 o/o Multiply the capital by the number of days, add up from right to left, add one half.

At 7 o/o Multiply the capital by the number of days, add up from right to left, add onne half and one fourth.

At 8 o/o Multiply the capital by the number of days, adé up from right to left, multiply by 2.

At 9 o/o Multiply the capital by the number of days, add up from right to left, multiply by 2, add the unit.

At 10 o/o Multiply the capital by the number of days, add up from right to left, multiply by 2, add one half.

Ex.—250—4 o/o
30- -days

7500
0,8332

At 5 o/o—250
30

7500
8332
2083

10415

At 6 o/o—250
30

7500
8332
4166

12498

At 7 o/o—250
30

7500
8332
4166
2083

14581

At 8 o/o—250
30

7500
8332
16664

At 9 o/o—250
30

7500
8332
16664
2083

18747

TABLE OF NUMBERS REPRESENTING THE RATES.

If you multiply the numbers representing the rates by the capital and then by the number of days, you will find the interest wanted, eight decimals should be pointed off in order to have the $ to the left and the cents to the right of the point.

If there are fractions as ¼ ½ ¾ to be added to the rate, add the corresponding number of these fractions to the simple rate.

If you want to find out interest at 2¼ o/o, take the number 5556, to wdich add 2430, in order to have the proper number for the multiplication by the capital and by the number of days, point off eight decimals and you have the interest wanted.

To find out interest at 10,11,and 12o/o, all you have to do is to double the number representing 5 o/o 5½ o/o, etc.

THE SIGN O/O MEANS PER CENT.

Rates.	numbers.	Rates.	numbers.
⅛ o/o	347	4¾ o/o	13194
⅜ o/o	1041	5 o/o	13889
¼ o/o	694	5¼ o/o	14583
½ o/o	1389	5½ o/o	15277
¾ o/o	2083	5¾ o/o	15972
⅞ o/o	2430	6 o/o	16667
⅝ o/o	1736	6¼ o/o	17361
1 o/o	2778	6½ o/o	18055
1¼ o/o	3472	6¾ o/o	18750
1½ o/o	4166	7 o/o	19444
1¾ o/o	4861	7¼ o/o	20139
2 o/o	5556	7½ o/o	20833
2¼ o/o	6250	7¾ o/o	21528
2½ o/o	6944	8 o/o	22222
2¾ o/o	7639	8¼ o/o	22916
3 o/o	8333	8½ o/o	23611
3¼ o/o	9028	8¾ o/o	24305
3½ o/o	9722	9 o/o	25000
3¾ o/o	10416	9¼ o/o	25694
4 o/o	11111	9½ o/o	26388
4¼ o/o	11805	9¾ o/o	27083
4½ o/o	12500